Real Lives

Victorian Town Children

Four real children, four different lives

Sallie Purkis

Contents

A & C Black • London

Life in Victorian towns

Victoria was queen from 1837 to 1901. During this period there were many changes in the way people lived. Britain was called 'the workshop of the world' because there were so many factories, making everything from engines to clothes. Lots of people moved from the countryside to work and live in towns.

Life in town was unpleasant compared with the countryside. There were not enough sewers to take away all the waste, and black smoke from factory chimneys polluted the air. There were beggars in the street, and pickpockets who stole from people walking by.

As well as people to work in them, factories needed materials such as cotton and iron to make their goods. These were brought into ports at London, Belfast, Liverpool and Glasgow. Railways were built at this time that made it easier to carry these

materials around the country. They also transported the goods made by the factories. Mining towns grew bigger as more coal was needed to fuel the machinery in the factories. The railways took the coal to where it was needed. Shipyards built steamships, which also needed coal to fire their engines, and which travelled to every country of the world.

New houses were built for the people moving into the towns. Poor people lived in small houses built close together near where they worked. They often had no running water, electricity or proper drainage, so as well as being overcrowded they were cold and unhealthy.

Families were larger in Victorian times than they are today. Mothers had a new baby every year, but many babies died very young. Little was known then about what causes diseases and how to control them. There were very few medicines and it was expensive to see a doctor, so most people were treated at home by their family.

Children often worked from a young age to bring in extra money, and also had lots of chores to do at home. Coal fires were used to heat water and to do the cooking, and everything was done by hand.

Rich people had very different lives. They built big homes and employed servants who worked long hours to serve the family, doing all the cooking and cleaning. Children from rich homes had no chores to do and spent most of their time in the nursery with their toys. They were often brought up by a nanny and taught by a tutor or governess. Some boys were sent away to boarding school, while girls went to day schools or stayed at home and learned how to play the piano, sing, dance and embroider. Parents were strict, expecting children to be seen and not heard. Rich children were taught to think about less fortunate children. They and their parents gave money to charities such as Doctor Barnardo's and the Salvation Army.

Most towns and cities had a park, laid out with flowerbeds and ponds, and many zoos were first opened in the 19th century. If they had any spare time, families walked in the park or visited the zoo. Adults with money to spare visited the theatre or music hall.

In this book you can read about four real children who lived in a town or city in Victorian times. Two of the families were rich and two were poor. Although they lived at the same time, their lives were very different. The stories of their lives have come from different sources of information, which you can read about on pages 4 and 5.

Thomas lived in a poor area of Glasgow. When he was ten he went to sea as a cabin boy, and later worked in America.

Fothergill lived in a large new house his father, a wealthy architect, built for the family in Nottingham.

Sarah lived in a poor slum area of London. Life for her and her family was a struggle and she had to work very hard.

Margaret's family was very wealthy. Her mother died when she was a baby, so she was brought up by a nanny.

How we know

A biography is the story of someone's life written by another person. A biographer can use many different sources of information to write the story. These are some of the sources of information we have used to find out about the lives of the four children in this book.

Buildings

Buildings can show us how people lived at the time they were built. Many of the buildings designed by Fothergill's father can still be seen today, although his home has been pulled down to make way for a new motorway. The Ragged School where Sarah and her sister went to school is a museum today.

Census returns

Every ten years every household in the country has to fill in a form giving the names of the people living there on census night. The information is kept private for 100 years, but we have been able to look at the forms for all the families in this book. The forms tell us how old the people were when the census was taken, and where they were born.

Graves

Graves often have information about the people who are buried there, such as the years they were alive. You can see Thomas's grave in the Southern Necropolis in Glasgow, and there is a memorial to Margaret in the Leicester Museum and Art Gallery.

Birth certificates

A birth certificate is an official form giving details of when and where a person is born and the names of their parents. A copy of everyone's birth certificate is kept in the Family Records Centre in London or in Register House in Edinburgh. This is a copy of Margaret's birth certificate. It gives her mother's married name and her maiden name (her surname before she married).

Written accounts

Written accounts can be found in diaries, letters, autobiographies and newspapers. When Margaret died, her half-sister, Bella, wrote an account of their childhood together. Fothergill's father kept a diary with details of his home and family, and Thomas wrote his autobiography just before he died. The information about the Jubilee fête in Hyde Park came from *The Times* newspaper for June 1887. Sarah's and Harriet's names were found in the registers of Copperfield Road Ragged School.

Photographs

Photography was invented in Victorian times and photographs show us how people dressed, travelled and lived then. Many photographs from these early days have survived and can be seen in local libraries. Some people have photographs of their Victorian ancestors in their family albums.

Margaret

Margaret came from a very wealthy family. Her mother died three weeks after she was born, but she lived happily in a large house in London with her father and her four half-sisters.

On 20 July 1870, a baby girl was born in London. Her father, John Gladstone, was a very wealthy Professor of Chemistry at London University. The baby, named Margaret after her Scottish mother, was strong and healthy, but she was cared for by the family nanny as her mother remained pale and ill in bed. Three weeks later, tragedy struck and Margaret's mother died.

There were no parties to celebrate Margaret's birth as the family had to go into mourning. In Victorian times it was the custom for the whole family to dress in black clothes for up to six months. There was a funeral procession from their house in Notting Hill, a fashionable district of west London. All the neighbours closed their curtains as a mark of respect as the coffin went past, carried in a hearse drawn by four horses with black plumes on their heads.

There were plenty of people to look after the new baby and to love her. John Gladstone had had four daughters with his first wife, who had also died, and they all lived at

A copy of Margaret's birth certificate. Her mother was already very ill in bed and died shortly afterwards.

home. The eldest Florence, was 15, Elizabeth was 12, Isabella nine and May seven. The family lived in a very large three-storey villa and, like other wealthy families in Victorian times, had eight servants, who also lived in the house. Part of the house was reserved for the children, who had a day nursery, a night nursery and a schoolroom. Nanny Dobson was in charge of Margaret and her sisters, and as they had no mother it was she who brought up the girls. There was also a nursery maid, Elizabeth George, who helped Nanny Dobson.

Mrs Gray, the housekeeper, ran the house. Mrs Watson was the cook and Hannah, the 16-year-old kitchen maid, worked under her. Hannah had to prepare the vegetables, wash the dishes and scrub the floor. A footman waited at table, and two housemaids did the housework, kept the fires burning with coal and attended the family if they rang one of the bells that were built into each room.

The coachman lived above the stables in the mews just outside. The Gladstones had their own carriage and a pair of horses to take them around London. Margaret and her sisters went to French conversation classes and to the dressmakers, to church and to visit relatives. The family travelled to the railway station in the coach when they went on holiday.

The family were looked after by a housekeeper and maids, who all wore special uniforms.

Like other large houses at the time, Margaret's house had a big garden. There was a mulberry tree under which Margaret and her sisters liked to play, and a greenhouse with a collection of exotic plants. The girls called the greenhouse 'the museum' because they kept their collection of seashells there, along with interesting gifts brought to the house by visitors. Margaret liked to go into the greenhouse with her sisters to admire all the lovely things it stored. As well as their own garden, the family could use the grassy garden in the square in front of the house. This was surrounded by a fence and had a locked gate.

The families who lived around the square each had a key to the garden gate, and sometimes Maggie, as Margaret was known, went there with her sisters and one of the servants. Here, they played or had a picnic with children from the other big houses surrounding the square. At Christmas time, Margaret and the other children acted in short plays that they performed for family, relatives, servants and friends.

Margaret had a happy childhood, but she was not spoilt. No sweets or rich food were served in the nursery, and in winter the rooms were often cold as there were only coal fires in the largest. Both Mrs Gray and Nanny Dobson strongly believed that children should not be fussed over. Every afternoon when Margaret was small she was taken out in her pram for fresh air.

As she grew older, Margaret was taken out with her sisters for walks along the Regent's Canal. This had been opened in 1820 as an important transport route. All sorts of cargo, from coal to textiles to cheese, was transported on barges along the canal.

Tutors and governesses taught Maggie and her sisters in their schoolroom every morning. They had lessons in reading, writing and arithmetic. They also learned some geography and history such as the names of countries around the world and the names of kings and queens. At the age of 12, Margaret was sent to a small private day school nearby. She wrote about her lessons in her diary. In the mornings she had arithmetic, French, grammar, history or geography lessons. The afternoons were spent drawing and painting, playing music and singing.

Margaret had to practise playing her piano every day at home. She also went to Sunday School, and when she was old enough she helped her sister to teach the younger children.

Although she did not see much of her father most days, Maggie had regular holidays with him. When she was younger he took her to Scotland to stay with her mother's family.

Later, her aunts and grandmother came to live in London and Margaret went to visit them on Saturday afternoons. Her aunts opened a photography studio and Margaret liked to visit them there. She loved looking through all the photographs they had taken. As Margaret grew older, her father took her abroad to Europe, when he travelled to attend scientific conferences.

When Margaret grew up

Margaret worked hard for people less fortunate than herself. She married a member of Parliament for Leicester called Ramsay Macdonald and had six children. She died when she was only 41. Later, her husband became the first Labour Party Prime Minister.

Fothergill

Fothergill lived with his family in a beautiful new house in Nottingham. He was sent to boarding school in London, but he did not enjoy it and returned to Nottingham as soon as he could.

Two days before Christmas in 1874, Samuel Watson was born at his family's new home in Nottingham. He was named after one of his grandfathers, but was always called by his second name, Fothergill, which was also his father's name. There were already four girls in the Watson family – Marian, who was five, Annie aged four, Edith aged three and Eleanor, just one. Two years after Fothergill, a brother, Forbes, was born, and another sister, Clarice, the following year.

In 1874 Nottingham was growing at an astonishing rate, with lots of new buildings going up. For people like Fothergill's father, who was an architect, this was an exciting time. He had plenty of work and earned a lot of money, so his family led a life of wealth and comfort.

Two years before the arrival of baby Fothergill, his father had designed a new house for the family. It was in the very latest style, with detailed brickwork, arched windows and a turret

Fothergill's family lived in this large house in Mapperley Road, Nottingham. Unfortunately it was pulled down in 1968.

roof. It was beautifully furnished with the best of everything.
There were huge fireplaces and modern gas lighting. The
curtains were made of rich velvet, with the furniture
upholstered to match. To help run the house the family
had a cook, a nursemaid, a housemaid and a governess.

Every morning Fothergill's father, smartly dressed, rode to
his architect's office in a horse-drawn cab. Fothergill and his
brother and sisters went to their spacious, specially built
schoolroom in the house, where the governess was in charge.
The maid lit the fire early in the beautiful fireplace, which
had hand-painted tiles designed by their father. The room
was cosy and warm by the time the children arrived. They
were taught reading, writing and arithmetic. They learned
prayers and poems by heart and read passages from the Bible.

Good manners were expected at all times, and Fothergill
and his brother and sisters had to arrive on time for the main
family meal, which was served at half past one. Everyone
had to say grace at the beginning and end of the meal.

Servants brought the food to the table and served it onto each person's plate. During the meal, Fothergill often had to answer questions from his parents about what he had learned that day.

Tutors visited the house on some afternoons to teach the children music, drawing, French and German. Fothergill was particularly good at drawing. He was also very interested in animals and birds. He loved his bird table and regularly put out food for the birds, especially in the winter. He also had some pet rabbits and guinea pigs, and when he was older he started to train a hawk to come back to him.

Sometimes the children were taken out by their parents. The girls went to take afternoon tea with friends of their mothers. Sometimes they visited poor families, taking them second-hand clothes for the children and food, such as pies baked by the cook. Fothergill and his brother were not expected to become involved in charity work. Sometimes in the summer, if their father was in a good mood, he would take the boys to the famous Trent Bridge cricket ground to watch the Nottinghamshire county cricket team play.

On Sundays, Fothergill went to church with the rest of his family and, as they grew older, the girls took turns teaching at the Sunday School.

Fothergill went on holiday once to Scotland with his family, and on other occasions they went to Great Malvern in Worcestershire and to Yorkshire. The family travelled on the latest invention – the railway. They went first to Nottingham Midland station where they had time to admire the huge steam engine which pulled the train. The fireman stoked up the fire in the cab and filled the boiler with water to get up a good head of steam. Then they all settled down in their carriage until they heard the guard blow his whistle.

They were off! The train seemed to fly through the countryside, although it only travelled at about 25 miles an hour. The family took their servants with them and stayed in rented houses. Fothergill loved to escape from the city and walk in the hills with his brother, going to the top of the Worcestershire Beacon, the highest point in the Malvern Hills.

In the
spring of 1880,
when Fothergill
was just six, there
was an exciting
family event. Without
telling them, his father had been making arrangements
for the family to have their own carriage. They were amazed
when it first arrived outside their home and could hardly
believe it was theirs, because although they were quite
rich they had never had a coach of their own. What a
magnificent sight it was!

Designed by their father, the inside of the coach had been
upholstered in green and scarlet. The harnesses for the
horses were silver plated, and rosettes and streamers were
attached to their bridles. The carriage was driven by a
coachman and groom, who wore matching green jackets
with bright red collars and red pocket flaps. Round their hats
they had a twisted silver cord.

After this, Fothergill and the other children, and even the
neighbours, liked to watch their father go down the road in

the carriage to his office every morning. He was always stylishly dressed and wore a top hat.

Fothergill's happy home life soon came to an end when he was sent away to a boarding school in London. He was only nine and was very unhappy at the thought of going, making himself ill with worry. However, his father was determined that he should go to a smart preparatory school, and spent a lot of money on the school fees.

Three years later, Fothergill was sent to Harrow, a famous school for boys. His father hoped he would go on to a university like most of the other pupils, but Fothergill was not happy at school and as soon as he was 16 he told his father he wanted to leave and return to Nottingham.

Fothergill and his brother were sent to Harrow School, where they had to wear school uniform like this.

When Fothergill grew up

Fothergill's father arranged for him to start work in an engineering firm in Nottingham. Later, he bought him a share in the firm. Fothergill left Nottingham when he married. He died before his father, when he was only 40.

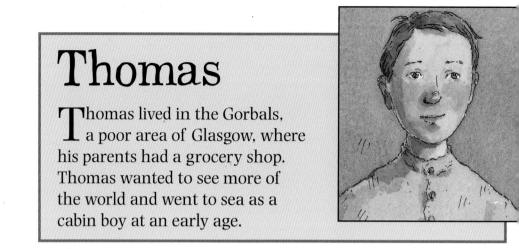

Thomas

Thomas lived in the Gorbals, a poor area of Glasgow, where his parents had a grocery shop. Thomas wanted to see more of the world and went to sea as a cabin boy at an early age.

Thomas was born in Glasgow on 10 May 1850. His mother, Frances, and his father, also called Thomas, were both Irish. After getting married, the Liptons had taken the boat across the Irish Sea and set up home in Scotland. They were poor people and had heard that there was a better chance of finding a good job in Glasgow than at home.

Thomas found work in a factory. Frances was pregnant and soon had a baby. They were very sad when he died shortly after he was born. A year later, tragedy struck again when their second son also died. At last, a year later, a third son, James, survived. They then had a daughter, Margaret, followed by Thomas, who was strong and healthy.

Photograph of Thomas at the age of 12.

Glasgow was the second largest city in the British Empire. It had iron works, factories, coal mines and shipyards. Every night fires from blast furnaces lit up the night sky and Thomas's room as he slept. Along the River Clyde were shipyards where hundreds of men worked building the steamships which sailed from the quayside to almost every country in the world. The men who owned these industries became very rich and lived in the fashionable west end of Glasgow. The Lipton family, however, like most of the workers, had to be content with a few rooms in a crowded tenement block.

Thomas's mother provided good, but simple, meals such as porridge, Scotch broth, scones and potato soup. She also made the children's clothes. In the evenings, Thomas and his brother and sister would sit round the fire and listen to their parents' stories about the home they had left behind in Ireland. As he grew up, Thomas learned the Irish songs and stories his mother sang to him. On Sundays the whole family went to church, just as their parents had done in Ireland.

The main street in the Gorbals area of Glasgow where Thomas's parents opened their first shop.

One day, Thomas's parents told the children that they had decided to do something adventurous. Instead of their father going out to work, the family would rent the ground floor of 13 Crown Street, the street where they lived, and turn it into a shop. A farmer from their home village in Ireland had agreed to supply them with ham, cheese and eggs which they would send on the steamer that travelled between Belfast and Glasgow.

The Lipton family would sell the produce, at a profit, in their new shop. They knew that they were taking a risk, and the whole family had to help. Thomas's job was to take a hand cart to the quayside every Monday afternoon, collect the food from Ireland when the steamship docked, and then take it back to the shop. He also helped his father keep the shop windows bright and clean, polish the wooden counter and deliver any orders customers asked for.

As well as working, Thomas went to school, even though it was not compulsory at the time. Half the children in Glasgow did not go to school at all, but Thomas's parents were keen for him to learn as much as he could. Thomas went to a church school called St Andrews, and every Monday his parents gave him threepence to pay the fees. Although Thomas tried hard, he was not a good pupil. He was always thinking about other things, such as the friends he played with in the street. They called themselves the Crown Street Clan. They raced around the streets and often fought with boys from other streets.

Most of all Thomas thought about the big ships he saw on the Clyde. Often the boat from Ireland was late, and then Thomas walked around the docks, looking at all the ships moored up, talking to the sailors and dock-workers. He always asked them where they had come from and where they were going next. He even bought a cheap map of the world to find the places they had been – China, India or Peru.

When he was nine, Thomas decided he had had enough of school. There were no laws about attendance at the time, and one day, without telling his parents, he skipped school and went into the city to look for a job. He soon noticed a board outside a shop which read 'Boy Wanted: Apply Within'. He walked in and spoke to the manager behind the counter who, without taking too much notice of him, said he could start at once. The hours were long and he had to work six days a week helping around the shop and running errands. His mother and father were anxious about him, but soon gave up trying to persuade him to stay on at school.

Thomas was restless and wanted to find out more about the world outside Glasgow. He was still very interested in ships, and even built a model, the *Shamrock*, when he was 11. He made the hull from the lid of an old wooden trunk and the sails from strong paper. The other members of his gang were so impressed that they built their own model ships, which they took to a

nearby field to race on the ponds that had formed in the holes left by old brick works.

When Thomas heard of a job going as a cabin boy on one of the Belfast to Glasgow boats, he went to sea for the first time. But he had even bigger plans. He wanted to cross the ocean to seek his fortune in America.

By saving a bit of money from his wages and the tips given to him by passengers, Thomas was gradually able to save enough to buy the cheapest ticket available. He said goodbye to his family and boarded a liner called the *Devonia*. Three weeks later, on his fifteenth birthday, his dreams had at last come true and he was looking for work in New York.

When Thomas grew up

One of Thomas's jobs in America was at a famous New York grocer's, where he learned more about shop keeping. He returned to Scotland and set up a chain of grocers' shops. Everyone soon knew about Lipton's brand of tea. He never married and when he died left most of his fortune to hospitals and schools for the people of Glasgow.

Sarah

Sarah and her family lived in Stepney, a very poor part of the East End of London. She went to a free school, but also had to work hard to earn money to help the family. Life was a struggle from day to day.

Sarah was born in one of the poorest parts of London. Her father, Thomas, was a labourer. He did not have a regular job, but took whatever work he could find, such as work at the docks, lifting heavy coal or rock on or off the barges.

Many poor families had to live in crowded buildings like this one in the East End of London.

Her mother, Harriet, took in work from the factories near where they lived. When Sarah was born, they already had four other children, three girls called Susanna, Harriet and Annie, and one boy, Thomas. Neither of Sarah's parents could read or write.

Sarah's home was in Regent's Court, not far from the Regent's Canal, where barges carried goods to and from the River Thames. It was not a comfortable place to live and some people called it a slum. Houses were built very close together, one row backed on to another and a narrow alleyway, called a court, separated them from the next block of houses.

Many families had to share the same house as they couldn't afford to rent more than two rooms. There were no taps inside the houses. Sarah had to help carry water for drinking or cooking from a standpipe in the court, but this

was not always turned on. There were no bathrooms or flushing toilets. Instead, Sarah and her family had to use a wooden box built over a pit, which was also used by every other family in the block. They collected rainwater in a tub to do the laundry, and threw dirty water from the kitchen into an open drain running through the court. They took household rubbish, including ash from the fire, to an ashpit near the toilet, but it was not cleared regularly and often overflowed. The area was smelly, and in hot weather it was full of flies. Many people became ill because of the germs.

Sarah's father went out every day to try to find a job. Her mother took in work which could be done at home, like making boxes for one of the local factories, or making paper bags, or paper flowers to decorate rich women's clothes and hats. She did not earn very much for each item and had to work very hard. Sarah and her sisters often helped her.

Sarah looked forward to lucky days when her father brought home money or the factory paid her mother. Then the family could have a real treat of a little meat, such as a chop, or some treacle to spread on their bread. On bad days they had potatoes, watery soup or porridge. Some days there was nothing in the larder at all. At night, Sarah slept on a mattress on the floor, which she shared with her brother and sisters in the same room as their parents.

Sarah never had new clothes. Her mother bought second-hand clothes that were sometimes little more than rags, and a lot of sewing had to be done at home to try to make them fit. Shoes were also a luxury. Each pair Sarah had was mended over and over again. Sometimes, her mother was able to ask for help from a charity that had collected money from rich people like the families of Margaret and Fothergill.

Every day Sarah and her brother and sisters were sent out to scavenge. They had to look out for anything lying around that could be useful for the family, like rotten fruit or vegetables left behind in the market. Even wooden boxes were taken home to be chopped up for firewood. Sometimes Sarah earned a penny or two running errands for stallholders on the market.

Sarah's parents wanted her and her brother and sisters to go to school, but most schools charged a small fee. However Copperfield Road Ragged School had been opened by Doctor Barnardo, who worked to help orphans and children with poor parents like the Boswells, and they went to this school for free.

The Doctor Barnardo charity also provided food and clothes for the pupils. Sarah arrived between 7 and 8 o'clock in the morning. She had to wash as soon as she arrived and put on the school clothes. She was then given a breakfast of watery cocoa and a large hunk of bread. At lunch time, she and the other pupils had a bowl of thick vegetable soup and bread dipped in milk.

Sarah was taught reading, writing and sums. She also learned to sing hymns, say prayers and learn passages from the Bible by heart. Copperfield Road School tried to teach the pupils some practical subjects that would help them when they grew up. Sarah and Harriet learned to sew, knit, wash clothes and cook.

One day Sarah always remembered was 22 June 1887. The whole country celebrated Queen Victoria's Golden Jubilee. All over London, flags and wreaths of flowers decorated the lampposts. Children were given a holiday from school and around 30,000 poor London schoolchildren were invited to a huge treat in Hyde Park in the West End of London. Sarah had never been so far away from home before.

In Hyde Park the children were given a paper bag full of good things. Inside was a meat pie, a bun, a piece of cake and an orange to eat, as well as a silver medal with the queen's head engraved on each side. There was ginger beer, lemonade and milk to drink. Afterwards they went to see the Punch

and Judy shows, puppet theatres, performing dogs, monkeys and ponies, coconut shies and lucky dips. At 4 o'clock the Prince and Princess of Wales arrived. Sarah lined up with the other children along the path to get a good view of the procession. At last the queen's carriage came into the park and the bands struck up with 'God save the Queen'. With a wave from the queen, the royal carriage moved on and out of the park. It was time for them all to go home.

When Sarah grew up

We do not know what happened to Sarah after she left school. She probably found work as a servant in the house of a rich family, where the skills she was taught at Copperfield Road would have been very useful.

Time line

National events

Personal events

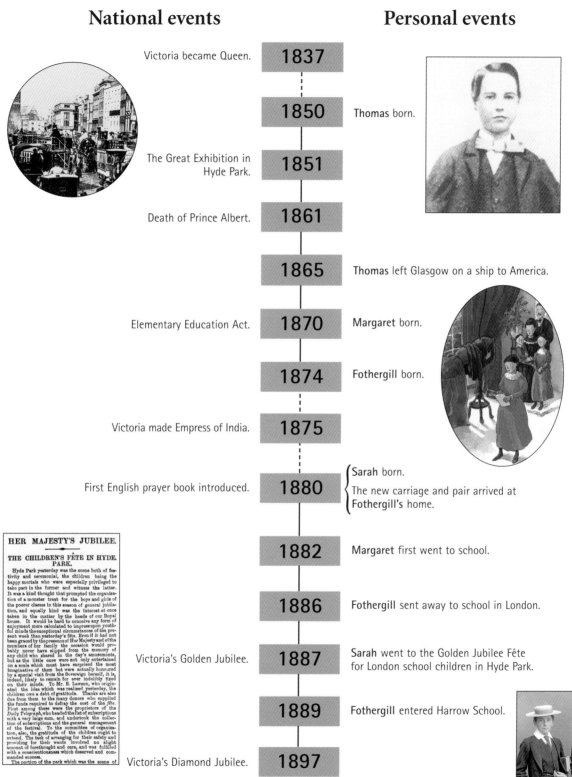

National events	Year	Personal events
Victoria became Queen.	**1837**	
	1850	Thomas born.
The Great Exhibition in Hyde Park.	**1851**	
Death of Prince Albert.	**1861**	
	1865	Thomas left Glasgow on a ship to America.
Elementary Education Act.	**1870**	Margaret born.
	1874	Fothergill born.
Victoria made Empress of India.	**1875**	
First English prayer book introduced.	**1880**	Sarah born. The new carriage and pair arrived at Fothergill's home.
	1882	Margaret first went to school.
	1886	Fothergill sent away to school in London.
Victoria's Golden Jubilee.	**1887**	Sarah went to the Golden Jubilee Fête for London school children in Hyde Park.
	1889	Fothergill entered Harrow School.
Victoria's Diamond Jubilee.	**1897**	

HER MAJESTY'S JUBILEE.

THE CHILDREN'S FÊTE IN HYDE PARK.

Hyde Park yesterday was the scene both of festivity and ceremonial, the children being the happy mortals who were especially privileged to take part in the former and witness the latter. It was a kind thought that prompted the organization of a monster treat for the boys and girls of the poorer classes in this season of general jubilation, and equally kind was the interest at once taken in the matter by the heads of our Royal house. It would be hard to conceive any form of enjoyment more calculated to impress upon youthful minds the exceptional circumstances of the present week than yesterday's fête. Even if it had not been graced by the presence of Her Majesty and of the members of her family the occasion would probably never have slipped from the memory of any child who shared in the day's amusements, but as the little ones were not only entertained on a scale which must have surprised the most imaginative of them but were actually honoured by a special visit from the Sovereign herself, it is, indeed, likely to remain for ever indelibly fixed on their minds. To Mr. E. Lawson, who originated the idea which was realized yesterday, the children owe a debt of gratitude. Thanks are also due from them to the many donors who supplied the funds required to defray the cost of the fête. First among these were the proprietors of the *Daily Telegraph*, who headed the list of subscriptions with a very large sum, and undertook the collection of subscriptions and the general management of the festival. To the committee of organization, also, the gratitude of the children ought to extend. The task of arranging for their safety and providing for their wants involved no slight amount of forethought and care, and was fulfilled with a conscientiousness which deserved and commanded success. The portion of the park which was the scene of

How to find out more

Visit the local history collection in your library

Ask to see any black and white photographs the library has collected of your town in Victorian times. It may have books about the town too, and a collection of old maps which will show how the town grew in size at different times.

Visit a museum

Most local museums have items on display from Victorian times. Ask if they have any mugs or medals given to children at the time of Queen Victoria's Golden or Diamond Jubilee.

Visit a cemetery

Victorian families often went for a walk round the local cemetery on Sunday afternoons. They liked looking at the inscriptions on headstones, as well as the enormous monuments wealthy people put up for their families.

Log on

Find out more about Victorian times on these websites.

www.raggedschoolmuseum.org.uk
You can see a picture of the objects given to the children who went to the Hyde Park Fête in 1887.

www.watsonfothergill.co.uk
You can read about Fothergill's father on this site and see pictures of many of the buildings he designed.

www.gorbalslive.org.uk
This is a site about the Glasgow Gorbals area, including memories of people who lived there.

www.victorians.org.uk
You can explore the daily lives of a Victorian family.

www.bbc.co.uk/schools/victorians
Activities, games and worksheets on the topic of Victorian children.

Things to do

Write about your life

Make photocopies of your birth certificate and photographs of yourself as a baby and of your family. Start to write about the homes you have lived in and any important events you have attended. Take new photographs of your school and the places you like to go, to make a record for years to come.

Family history

Interview your grandparents about their grandparents, who they were and where they lived. Can anyone in your family go back over a hundred years and write down information for you about your family in Victorian times? Make a time line showing the dates of any births and deaths that you can find out about.

Imagine a conversation

Both Sarah and Margaret lived near the Regent's Canal in London, but they never met. Margaret collected money for Doctor Barnardo's Charity and Sarah received food and clothes from the fund. Make up a conversation they might have had if they had met.

Write a newspaper article

Read about the big party in Hyde Park that Sarah and her sister went to for Queen Victoria's Jubilee. Write an account of the day for a newspaper.

Become a researcher

Find out more about Dr Barnardo, who founded the Copperfield Road Ragged School, and about the work done by the Doctor Barnardo's Charity today. Make a list of popular charities such as Children in Need, which collect money for good causes today. What is different about the way we give today from the way people gave in Victorian times?

Book list

Penelope Harnett, *A Day in the Life of a Victorian Child*, Heinemann. This is a version of everyday life gathered from lots of different sources.
Claire Seymour, *Ragged School, Ragged Children*, a Ragged School Museum book.
Pamela Horn, *The Victorian Town Child*, Sutton Publishing Ltd.
Laura Wilson, *Daily Life in a Victorian House*, Hamlyn. This is about a home like Margaret's and Fothergill's.

Places to visit

Ragged School Museum, 48–50 Copperfield Road, London E3 (0208 9806405)
This is where the Boswell children went to school. In the museum you can find out more about the pupils and where they lived, and take part in activities organised by the museum.

The Mitchell Library, North Street, Glasgow G3 7DN (0141 2872999)
This has a special Sir Thomas Lipton Collection, with many photographs of his life.

The Tenement House Museum (0141 333 0183) and the People's Palace Museum (0141 5540223)
These museums both have displays on homes in Glasgow.

Linley Sambourne House, 18 Stafford Terrace, London W8 (0207 6023316)
Here, the original decoration and contents of a middle-class family house have been preserved.

Index

Acknowledgements

I would like to thank the following people and libraries for their help: Margaret Juett, Liz Braby, Ragged School Museum, Nottingham City Library, National Library for Scotland and the British Library.

Photographs: British Newspapers Library Archive: 5m; Harrow School: 17; Ingatestone Antiques 5b; National Monuments Record Centre, Swindon: 4t, 12; Popperfoto: 8; Southern Necropolis Research: 4b; The Family Records Centre: 5t, 6; The Mitchell Library, Glasgow: 18, 19; Tower Hamlets Local History Library and Archives: 2, 24. t=top; m=middle; b=bottom.

This edition 2007
Published 2004 by A&C Black Publishers Limited
38 Soho Square, London W1D 3HB
www.acblack.com

ISBN 978-0-7136-8826-9

Copyright text © Sallie Purkis, 2004
Copyright illustrations © Anna C Leplar, 2004

A CIP record for this book is available from the British Library.

Printed in Singapore by Tien Wah Press (Pte) Ltd

A&C Black uses paper produced with elemental chlorine-free pulp, harvested from managed sustainable forests.